INDIGO, ELECTRIC, BABY

First published in 2020 by
The Dedalus Press
13 Moyclare Road
Baldoyle
Dublin D13 K1C2
Ireland

www.**dedaluspress**.com

ISBN 9781910251690 (paperback)

Dedalus Press titles are available in Ireland
from Argosy Books (www.argosybooks.ie) and in the UK
from Inpress Books (www.inpressbooks.co.uk)

Printed in Ireland by Digital Print Dynamic

Cover design: Pat Boran

The Dedalus Press receives financial assistance from
The Arts Council / An Chomhairle Ealaíon.

INDIGO, ELECTRIC, BABY

ENDA COYLE-GREENE

Waterford City and County
Libraries

DEDALUS PRESS

ACKNOWLEDGEMENTS & THANKS

Acknowledgements are due to the following publications and radio programmes where a number of these poems, or versions of them, originally appeared: *Abridged; Crannóg; Mezzo Cammin; Orbis; Oxford Poetry; Poetry Ireland Review; Spolia; Sunday Miscellany; The Honest Ulsterman; The Irish Times; The Yellow Nib* and *Visions International.*

Poems are also included in the following anthologies: *Reading the Future: New Writing from Ireland,* edited by Alan Hayes (Arlen Press, 2018); *The Lea-Green Down: Irish Poets Respond to Patrick Kavanagh,* edited by Eileen Casey (Fiery Arrow Press, 2018); *The Sea: Irish Poets in Support of the RNLI,* edited by Gene Barry (Rebel Poetry, 2015); *Sunday Miscellany: a selection from 2004–2006,* edited by Cliodhna Ni Anluain (New Island, 2006)

'At Floraville' was commissioned for permanent display at Floraville Park, Skerries, Co. Dublin. 'Blind' won the Short Poem category at the Poetry on the Lake Festival, Orta San Julio, Italy, 2013.

The author would like to thank the following:

Pat Boran for his empathetic attention to the work and always-clear eye; Raffaela Tranchino for much more than a phone call. Paula Meehan, Theo Dorgan, Aidan Mathews, Leontia Flynn, Mairide Woods, Pádraig J. Daly, Tony Curtis, Patricia Kennan, and Oonagh Catchpole: for their generosity.

Susan McKay, Ernestine Woelger, Linda McLoughlin, Aileen Morrissey, Rosemary Murray, Catherine Sheehan, Teresa Bissett, and Marie Bashford-Synnott: for walking the beach with me in all weather. Ivy Bannister, Beth O'Halloran, Julie Cruickshank, Antoinette McCarthy, and Maggie O'Dwyer: for wise advice on the words.

Clíona Uí Thuama and Robbie Ryan: for permission to quote from Gloria de Carlos V by Thomas MacGreevy, and to Susan Schreibman for her kind assistance in arranging this.

The Tyrone Guthrie Centre at Annaghmakerrig: for being my home from home and the birthplace of many of these poems. Fingal County Council Arts Office for an Artists' Support Scheme Award in 2016.

Vanessa, Lawrence, Frank, Annabel, Bernadette, Peter, and Donal: you know why.

Contents

⁀)

INDIGO

ELECTRIC

BABY

i.m. Debi O'Hehir

Silver Blue,
Gleaming blue,
Gold,
Rose,
And the light of the world
— Thomas MacGreevy

Indigo

Easterly

What can it do, the sea,
in its own stony bed
with no one but me
awake and listening?

Turning over
and over, scored
by an easterly,
it roars.

Bruise

This is none of my business
but I have to go over and ask
if you are OK —
you and the boy (two, maybe
three at most) who clings
to your coat and howls
as the train sways
over the Loopline Bridge.

You'd started the palaver
of gathering, he must have let go
of your grip and tripped;
I've been there myself
in what now seems like
someone else's life.
But no, no, I didn't see
what happened —

all I heard was metal,
a slur of feet and then
your voice, the grief
that filled it as you cried,
He's hurt his eye …
I'd been miles away
inside a book
across the aisle

from you, your child
and the young man at the door,
who waits for you and blames you
with his silence. Glowering
in that tender space

on the boy's right eyelid,
the bruise blooms in colours
which owe nothing

to the sun this mid-March
afternoon, or last night's sky —
there's no resemblance
to a jewel owned by a king,
or a feather on a rain-sleek slate,
neither hint nor tint of the cloak
worn by God's mother
in every known painting.

I attempt to offer words
but the doors are opening
now, you need to leave.
Swooping back to lift
and take the boy, your man
leaves you to struggle,
sobbing like the child
you'll always be;

as much a baby
as the baby in the buggy
who's cocooned in pink,
asleep. I see her only
when you turn
towards the gate,
as you're all disappearing
into something ruined.

Indigo, Electric, Baby

The signal slips through
static, but I know

he's blue, that *fear gorm*
on the radio:

one word wrong
in the Irish tongue

conflates an alias
the devil might have

sweltered under back in days
before religion gripped.

He's playing music
with a curious plural

and, though I'm thirteen,
fourteen maybe, tuned

to cerulean, cyan,
cobalt, navy, manganese,

indigo, electric, baby —
colours I could touch

with a brush
slurred by water,

or feed to a needle
through its always-open eye —

I know blue can be black
as the dust-cut deal

sealed by dying
daylight in his song.

I know blue is a mood
no one chooses,

that it's composed
of bass rise, treble fall,

I know too
that what you name the shade

won't matter,
it will always call.

That Blue Time

It's the middle of the night, that blue time
disquieted by the phone in the hall,
so I don't move until I have to
turn and face the worry

he's been putting on the car's back seat
for weeks to bring to work with him,
and carries home again curled
at the edges like an uneaten lunch.

But what he says makes all the sense
of hieroglyphics cut into a cave wall
in Egypt, or an algebraic theorem
only ticked correct because

I'd learnt the formula by heart.
We drive to collect her. She stands
as we are shown into a room that's bare-
bulbed, fizzed with electricity.

While the village on the hill sleeps
on through other people's lives,
she explains how she'd got lost
and would have stayed

lost had the taxi man she'd flagged
decided otherwise. People are kind,
in the main, frangible as glass,
and it is years before

I need to know this.

Silveracre

for Bernadette

i

On the oldest map,
in jaded letters, spindly-

inked along a river's tributary,
I've found the Pin Mill:

even the sound is silver.
Pins pinned silk

swirled in crinolines, ribbons
on bonnets, a maid's plain

apron to its proper place, until
tin turned to flour, time climbed

and the high, dark interior grew
light as the roof blew out

to meet the crows. I've been told
how in the years before,

when rows of cottages were built
for the workers, ample

gardens meant for self-
sufficiency, nothing sown

in that ground flourished, pins
splintered the potato crops.

ii

The cottages filled
with the children of children

with memories sloughed
off the memories of others,

the mill its own ghost;
on a left-over slope

a man stopped and imagined
mortar, bricks.

So no, it's not a townland,
that name I had forgotten

until now, when you said it:
four syllables, the sound of silver

tilled. It survived for a while
on letters, postcards, bills, its glitter

flickered on the second line
of our first address.

Power Cut

Lightning stretched the night before we left
so we could see for miles beyond our garden
to the Hellfire Club's blunt stump, cut
out ragged-black against the sky behind the house,
past the field we'd run through to the only power
we thought could ever pulse between our walls.

Not that we ventured far beyond those walls —
six feet of brick at back, at right, at left,
our hail-rain-sun parameters of power,
the boundaries of our planet, our back garden.
Years before, a hand had drawn that house,
had numbered it on paper which was cut

then folded, filed inside a vault where air was cut
on plans for elevation, roof and party walls
we shared with strangers. A lighthouse
keeper, old, retired to shore, lived on our left —
no children shrieked like gulls in his neat garden.
Our neighbours to the right craved power,

had 'notions', but owned nothing of the power
that acres bring; they had all we had, a cut
of squared-off, hedge-edged garden,
or their land, as they'd yell across the wall
behind us (an errant ball could not be left).
Although we never stood in either house,

we'd long worked out how each house
mirrored ours, with rooms, like power
arranged in different ways. In the hours left
to us that final night we knew we'd cut

our lives into before and after bedroom walls
we'd crayoned on, a swing-swung-over garden.

When the storm stopped at the garden,
as its fury crashed down on our house,
our mother stumbled, clutched the wall
of clothes she'd ironed to pack; the power
faltered, fitted as flashed zigzags cut
that summer's famous heat. Left

not ready yet for new walls or new gardens,
in the morning we left nothing in the house
but dust, the door was shut, the power cut.

If, in Moving

Mistakes can be made
when lonely dogs bark
out of the darkness,
their bluff called
as you go past —
a star can be confused
with a plane full of strangers,
streetlights,

stemless, drift —
but if, in moving
what is there stays
fixed in poses
you might struggle
to unscramble,
if you choose to turn
towards the sea —

four islands night-snuffed
as you face the restless
red eye of the lighthouse —
the snarl of cars,
the lamentations of a train,
begin their fade;
even half-aware
you'll hear

the riff of wave on sand,
the top-note kick and slap of shoe
that keeping pace with you
is only you
insisting, *Yes*

you can,
you can,
you can …

A Sky Full of Noise

I mean to say something
about a fox I saw, mangy
with the task of being
urban as he padded through
the car park's gravel
in an inference of dust.

I could describe the tree —
trinkets are tied to it
and bouquets laid
by people my age
who were nearer your age
on the night that singer died.

But then, it's just a tree,
the fox is just a fox,
and in high late summer
there's a sky full of noise
as the flight path to and from
this city won't shut up.

Yes, yes, I intend to mention
this, that, whatever —
maybe when I get the guts
to let you know how much
we need to speak,
I might.

Friday, Saturday, Sunday, City

i

Friday finds us closer
to strangers

only inches away
beyond glass,

gone as soon
as they arrive

on the pavement
outside

in their own strange lives.

ii

Saturday could be spent
just meeting ourselves, ghosted

in shop windows;
but we lose the afternoon

to a gallery and all those faces
faced with an amalgam

that's as complex or as simple
as our conversation later

in the brittle glint of spring.

iii

Sunday pulls the door
behind us, closes

on last orders
and that young girl drinking

with a man who's pretending
to be drunk; in the rain

you hail a taxi, my lift arrives,
and I look back at you through glass

the wipers can't quite dry.

Blind

What you can't see has woken me, takes over
when I spool the blackout back into wherever night is
dyed by day.

But all I know of happiness is that its bones are startling,
simple as the sunlight billowing through cotton
on an always-open window:

spilled across a page, a poem, it drenches
black and white, it shows me everything
in gold.

Electric

The Weather on the Streets

I deluded myself I wouldn't get wet
as the sky flew, slack with rain-seed;
a busker sang of love, love and yet
more love, being all a body needs

as the sky flew, slack with rain-seed.
I went to buy a tidy black umbrella
(more love being all a body needs)
the singer singing *a cappella*

I went to buy a tidy black umbrella,
lying in my head with the refrain
(the singer sang it *a cappella)*
I stumbled in my heels in drains.

Lying in my head with the refrain
through hailstones melting, big as hearts,
I stumbled in my heels in drains,
I told myself it couldn't start.

Through hailstones melting big as hearts
a busker sang of love, love. And yet
I told myself it couldn't start.
I deluded myself. I wouldn't get wet.

The Blue Album — Eleven Small Self-Songs

INTRO

Saturday, a man's voice
spliced into this bar tonight
says something I can't answer,
belonging as I do to him
in air I moved through once,
twig-thin, staccato-heeled, unclear.
Lights falter as the band begins
to tune small self-songs, notes
found somewhere earthed
in breath. He's telling me
I haven't changed,
I turn around until he's facing
somebody not there.

1

A piano played
the way a stream plays
over stones, a flow through
the notes like poetry, a *Lied*
to the muse, to music.

A closed door and a long wait,
tired, hungry now yet patient
on a broad bench with a shine
as high as *C*.

An empty landing in a Georgian house.
A quiet child, too much so.
My mother's voice: soprano,
mezzo.

2

'Snot green'? This sea steals colour
from the sky, the light seems
buttered as the vowels I taste
when I say *California*.

The funfair's music breeze-drowned
now, the town receding in a mist
the church spires spike,
I choose small stones to skip
across a universe of drifts;

mapped by a splash, each
stows a story all its own,
God only knows
what mine will be.

3

It has no purpose, the frisbee, except to fly
between us while the sea lays down
its own persistent riff behind our house —

a summerhouse, essentially concrete
skimmed on cardboard layered with paint;
snow seeped through the roof in winter,

but primed for its element, fooled
by an afternoon in May, we twist-leap, glide,
eye-follow air-sliced arcs into a weightlessness

we've set to music, each game
timed to last until we flip
the record over,

play the other side.

4

He doesn't notice
the cold, the loss
of almost everything
he'd owned, viewed
from his open door
the Mournes rise crystalline
across the grey-washed bay
and in the house the radio plays
a song sung by a daughter.

He is listening as we all would
were we able to hear air,
or defer to a moment
before it's gone.

5

Placed by a stranger
whose cool gaze insinuates
love, here in my own town
behind a tall window, I'm lost
as the night that light has effaced
on the roofscape, the mountains,
beyond; up on this floor

that song on my radio
is old, and all wrong —
far from late, it's too early,
the morning so still
it's like no one could be busy
being born.

6

Outside a room in the hospital
where no one goes home —
a narrow corridor, a row of doors,

it's dark but still not quite
the dead of night. Yet
what will be remembered most

is this, this moment
and the sound of being alone —
my own voice rising

as he lies down with the ghosts,
an endless echo on that song
about a blackbird,

learning notes.

7

Uneasy suddenly, driving home
too soon, what could I know
that music will not soothe —
what makes me choose to sing
a prayer not meant but still sent
a cappella to pin wings
on to an angel set for flight?

Tall trees stand sentinel all the way
to the Cross. Tonight goes by
already scored by absences,
no orchestras, no choirs;
inside two hours
my mother will have died.

8

A name they've saved for us is 'Doom and Gloom,'
but I won't dwell on why or which applies
to whom; instead, I'll backtrack to a day
after Christmas, a taxi to the races
when those two cousins were our children still.

The driver, surly, racked his radio past loud
when it came on — that song, turned
on an utterance concerned with *nothin'*
and what, if anything, can be done about it,
which we hit, on the beat. *Whoa, ooh, ooh*

(but no couplet) must be my reply it seems,
this being one line short of a sonnet,
and us one sister shy of the Supremes.

9

This shouldn't be about
the song:

it kicks into a verse which pin-sticks
tears each time I've listened since
    we heard it first, stopped
    at the lights outside Drogheda.

Nor should it be about
where I did not learn how to drive:

— in the suburbs, someone's mother's car
    keys grabbed.

It shouldn't be about
the red-to-green, that town receding,

or a child, grown up and leaving.

10

... a ballerina but the block shoes bit,
an actor, dress designer, could have been a vet,
unshakeable on Shakespeare, Mahler, Yeats or Plath,
a pianist, a union rep (I could have been part cat).
I could have been a singer, could have been a song,
a beach on Achill Island, a lake in Monaghan.
I could have been unhappy, could have been
a fool, could have been a worker,
could have stayed in school.
I could have cursed my plight.
I could have missed this light.
I could have been
none of these things first.

11

On a road that flows past rust-
green trees and shallow fields
where small lakes shape-shift
in response to rain, I'm singing
from a place usually danced to —
with my daughter before breakfast,
say, or another crazy poet
at a *metaphoric* four a.m. —

I'm singing out of somewhere
deeper than the beat my heart gives me
no choice except to keep, driving
this song's piano-cascade chorus
with my loudest voice.

Flowers Found

He thinks he hears it in the din
made by his worker bees
and their lone drone,

in the fricative *slip* of nylon
over sweat, someone is humming
'Joe Hill'.

With no windows, one door,
in a room without weather
the other bees seethe;

in the absence of a queen
she has been chosen
although he owns the floor

and the whole world
balances its cold bowl of blue
while they calculate

the hours until lunch.
When the humming one rises —
gracile wings unfurled

at last, her coat off its hook
in the cloakroom's gloom —
she'll fly

into elements that blaze, sip
pollen from flowers found
on Dawson Street,

pressed in the pages of a book.

Full Moon Over Palmerston Road

Through all the time since then I see him there,
as cool as when he didn't judge the anguished
state of me, of other friends long vanished.
Terry with the Jesus eyes, the wavy hair
of painted saints, still walks as if on air
or water to the girl who banished
other girls, the pretty one who vanquished
talk of rights and wrongs with money, care.

But how were we to know that drifting on
in our unguided lives we'd never trace
our reasoning that night? We watched the sky
hold up a moon transfigured. While it shone
above the roofs its gentle, wise man's face
was only that, the almost-oldest lie.

The Marionette Maker

after the installation by Janet Cardiff and George Bures Miller
— Palacio de Cristal, Parcque del Retiro, Madrid

Her hands and feet look cold
in this heat, pearl-spun,
her gown's placid overlay
makes her slow pose amorphous
as the long hair streeled
across her shoulders,
vulnerable arms.

Behind a window in a caravan that's beige,
bland, beached on blocks and bellied
in a crystal dome, she sleeps
as I keep watch,

not really sure if she's unreal
or who's been charmed.

Before the sharp fall down from dawns and sunsets,
brittle stars and warm rain, clouds, seasons of birdsong
flew around them, part of a forest's plenitude;

and though I'll never speak their language, let alone try
those arpeggios he plays behind her at a doll's piano
on a stage cut into the caravan's flank,

she turns the face she owns now on me: painted
eyes and angry brows, a crimsoned hinge that opens, sings
how they were pinned against the world by wind once,

not by strings.

The murmurings begin: ululations maybe, back-swarmed
thunderclaps, waves of bomber jets and tune-scraps,

despite this midday's stubborn glaze they've come
from all night's worst assumptions. I can't shake the shapes

huge siren sounders phrase; filling air to where it's stopped
they follow me, alive as anything that breathes

or doesn't breathe or has been thought-
hacked here through silicone, hatched by wood.

The caravan is packed with stacked books, dangling pens,
an open tin congeals beside a sink, a peeled-off face
stares up at manic melds, nimble-limbed and featureless.

Behind a window there's an old man, almost life-size, over-
combed and hunch-slumped at a table laid with bones
and half a bird's white skull:

he mutters, groans, but keeps re-making notes
I know he'll never change.

Invaders on Wardour Street

Should we have stayed at home and thought of here?
— Questions of Travel, Elizabeth Bishop

Blurred
by day-to-day
where days herd

other days to Friday,
shutters down, all late
clubs closed, we step away

outside ourselves, inchoate
on Wardour Street.
Articulate,

though nothing's neat,
just held together
incomplete

as weather,
some cling to hope,
the thing with feathers;

others, tugged by dope
or drink, the slow
run out of rope

on nights like this in Soho
know it's a bed,
a place to go.

Jinking, giddy, self-led
through sad heart-
light neon bled

in gutters, drains, a part
of us already armed,
apart

from all that's harmed
and left us
charmed

perhaps, not dangerous,
we've been remade
anonymous.

In the hot arcade
the last machine
plays ceaselessly relayed

invaders, cruel, obscene,
bite-sniping on a whey-faced
screen —

tired now, spaced,
we are almost as alien,
equally displaced.

Brixton Triptych

The street is quiet in the morning
in the middle of July, at its quietest
on a Sunday while the whole world prays
or sleeps or overlooks the bus stop
opposite the squat. A woman waiting
crooks one knee and settles on a pose
to ease the load on her poor feet.
Matching her dress her hat is a garden
loud with flowers; iterated on the pavement
as her shadow she is ageless,
colour-bled.

CENTRE

Too red, too much of it, the girl's hair
falls just-so over her shoulders
while she concentrates on pulling
petals off a rose; afternoon slumps.
In a park that appears to be otherwise
empty, eyes shut against the sun,
at his end of the bench a boy becomes
forever young. He is feeling the heat
as an overheard, over-dubbed,
double-tracked beat
the photographer froze.

RIGHT

Composed as much of dust as air
there's just enough light to go around
a cat, more black than white, nameless now;
the floorboards are bare,
the curtains mere flimflam
tacked up and transient as days.
Framed by the window
and fronted by smoke, a slurred line
of attics and chimneystacks,
the street is like what happened next:
there.

Break

A thought idles
while the engine turns over
and the indicator ticks
    decision   decision

With so much blue
still to be filled
the sky finalises
an arrangement of clouds

as the traffic queues   But
you're not moving anywhere
until that break
which just won't wait

for one more breath

Baby

Charm

In the garden this morning
a trail of entrails leads me
to a tibia

the cat has whittled, gleaned
as far as what might be
a charm

conferred after a warning
never heard. *General
all over Ireland*, rain

has washed, not cleaned
a rabbit's foot, collateral
still furred.

Notes to Self in Relation to Biography

Once the initial stitch is snipped, ripped, worried
into looseness, are you invited to go deeper?
Beckoning from photos, shutter-stuck and locked
with tabulated smiles, the eyes aren't really readable,
another layer slicks a trail, rain-marbled, oiled;

there'll be backdrops, props, the kicked-up dust
of years, months, weeks, days, hours, minutes,
seconds spent as money, breath. Death,
on whatever page it lies, won't wear a face,
so don't assume to be much wiser. Take cognisance

of weather patterns as you smooth the creases
that occlude a townland small enough for you
to blink through, somewhere named for someone
who stopped long enough to carve a mark in tree bark.
Look — a footprint's muddied there, afford it nothing

less than the attention you should give to air
before you call on relatives and then remember
friends aren't strictly ethical; they should be listened to
like neighbours. Devious and innocent as any life is
being shunted between dates, it's rarely anywhere

you'll search for it, the wrong keys blistering the self-
same precious fist you lifted first through trust
towards the start of touch. In your heart
you know it's love and only love that will explain
us.

Visitors, Kidney Ward

I opened my eyes
again, certain I had died,
that what might have been
a lie was the truth. Gowned
in sky, sky-veiled and silent,
a flutter of women fussed
around the Virgin

while a bell sang something
jangled. I watched them
as they drifted and left
space for her, all solicitous
grace and vows taken
on the basis of the now
which is breath.

Later, you came in,
you brought my hairbrush
and my toothbrush, nothing
of much use for suffering.
Yet I still see you, hunkered —
our faces level, both of us
too young — I see my father,

blessed, blessed man,
walking through the ward
with that day's *Irish Times*
in one hand, cradling
a bag, split open, far too thin,
brimming with oranges
bought on Moore Street.

Window Seats

After he had scraped the block,
swept the floor and shut the shop,
he counted out the takings
listening to Radio Three.
He knew all about Sibelius,
Beethoven, Bach, Puccini,
Verdi and, especially, Wagner,
he didn't have much time
for Mozart, Chopin, Mahler.

Once, I saw him naked to the waist,
trouser braces trailing George Webb shoes,
stirring molten fat for the soap factory
in Dún Laoghaire. It was late.
We should have been at home by then,
the car safely bedded in the suburbs,
tea's debris still on the table,
television's fables black and white
behind a snow-blind screen.

My homework done, I drew on paper
used for swaddling steaks and mince,
the hearts on which he'd later make me mark
the price, after I had weighed them.
Outside, the Corporation truck sucked up
abandoned apples, pears, bananas
slimed like spit; lettuce leaves were
skirts cast off by fairies,
watered silk.

Don't call me uncle, doll, his youngest brother said —
it made him feel as old as the old man

I imagined him to be. Then, like Frank Sinatra
he would flick his cigarette away

between stiff fingers, way before the tip,
as if there were plenty more, there

where that had come from.

Two fire grates breasted the weather
on the shoe shop's beam-propped wall;
he always parked the car there.

We'd walk towards it, crossing first
to Burke's. Brownly invisible, I drank
red lemonade, he sank a pint

before he let our money slide
down the cool, tight throat
of the bank's night safe.

Saloon put me in mind of flouncy ladies
slinging whiskey back in stubby tumblers;
I never noticed that they'd left an *O* out
when they'd written it on glass below
the profile etched on Knox's door;

I looked through her onto Henry Street.
Darkness filled her in and swelled
the time I counted in the split ends
peeled apart to see if I was loved,
not loved. I waited

while the door behind me opened just enough
to let a laugh escape the smoky steam,
and someone else's air of beauty
passed me on the stairs.

I could see the stars catch fire
between cold chimneys. I could see

the moon rise up above the roofs.
Hard cash handed over, I could see

the plums she wanted weren't
the ones she'd bought. I could see

that they were soft and had been taken
from behind the stall. I could see

her skim each passing window
for its thin, reflected lie. I could see

what she could never see —
the light, already dying

in her eyes.

Thirst slaked, the *beardy man*
embraced his brown-bagged,
strangled bottle, folded

at the neck, the knees, heeling
over on the street, he stretched out
on a sheet of pee.

He'd made his bed, she told us
children not to look. Trying hard
we didn't step on lines —

one, two, three, we jumped
the grass the cracks spat up;
gaping at his black-mawed flies

we straddled cellar gratings
I was always sure would open wide
and swallow us.

On Moore Street
one by one
each light went out,

reeling gulls culled fish-
less heads in still-sea-reeking ice
the traders left to melt.

She fussed in high-heeled shoes
from Paris, carried shopping bags
that rustled loud as money.

He balanced books and papers, struggled
with the keys that rang like gaolers'
as he locked the shop.

When we were all there
in the car we sat behind them, fighting
over window seats.

Certain Birds

for Vanessa and Lawrence on their wedding day

Love should always be
like certain birds in flight,
what some describe
as never-music
feathered on a sky
that only hears it sweeter,
kinder, even named and mated
as the black-blue crows
at home in your new garden.

But you know this,
as you have always known
while growing nearer
to this day,
those *white birds*
on the foam of the sea,
their song insistent and as clear
as *all the birds of Oxfordshire*
and Gloucestershire.

The Tilt of the Wind

I've heard it told that when they go
so too will this whole world,
and now I'm finding out
about the first bee of summer —
the fat one that astonishes, lost
and panicked on my windowsill.

Brought by someone smarter in a glass
out to the garden, she thrashed the sky
while it was lifted from her, in the moment
when our tawny cat, all claws
and neatness stored within
black feet, pounced.

The bee spun in the sun, tried
her wings in the tilt of the wind,
but fell back, shivered,
curled, and couldn't rise
until I righted her
with the inky end of my pen.

At Floraville

The Pony Daly leans against a wall
in a photograph taken at Floraville;
stepped back from the footpath, the house
behind him has an eyeless, quiet look.

But Floraville was rarely that —
notes drifted into Strand Street from the hall
where the Graduates practiced, toes tapped
in *céilí* time at May Dillon's classes,

and on certain, thought-of-ever-after nights,
floorboards hopped and jittered, long
marriages were sparked. At Floraville
rooms filled like tides

until the Annex burnt and the house fell
into emptiness; on the lane the cottage
brimmed with weeds, a higher wall
was built around a secret.

Flowers are seeded now at Floraville,
waves are mapped and new trees grow
where children play among the ageless
patterns made by names.

Underground

And if your name is shy enough to slip back
through the closing door as you slide in,
 it might come to me later. Your face
 is a Venn diagram of features

wiped off other faces, out of place
on you somehow, and somewhat lost —
a fish in fog perhaps, or a fox
bin-rootling in a forest of gardens

every nerve and follicle intent on a box
once filled with chicken wings,
the skirmish preceding the kill
greased there like a memory inherited.

Your man is slightly older and still
wears a patina of handsome; that cravat,
the tilted hat, an ambience of tweed
and owning-his-own-air stance

makes you embrace an urgent need
to claim him, faults included, on a Tube
packed, oddly for this hour, with a crush
of stoic Londoners. As you both sway

your gaze absolves him in a rush
of lust. We're all soggy-silent but you rustle
in a dress my daughter, almost opposite me,
will call *puffy* — taffeta, the stiff stuff

of a ball gown cut down to graze the knee
you expose as he makes a scene of seeing
a free seat and drags you to his lap
while his eyes avoid the thighs

of the girl who strap-hangs in the gap
between us. I'm trying hard not to
glance towards my family, but oh —
the glamour! Fur, black stockings, seal-slick

patent sling-back sliding off a pointed toe
from which it dangles. The train groans
through the tunnel on this, the oldest line
in the city, as both of you keep doing

that thing to which the famous incline —
which I've seen many times although
they will insist on just how much they hate
being recognised —

antennae steadied, rapt, as they await,
no, they expect, our mad reactions.
I suspect that I might be the only one
who could oblige tonight

but I'll be damned if I do, fun
as this must be for you, me, my beloveds,
on our way to a party in the West End,
(my niece's twenty-first, actually)

but that would seem to depend
on how one looks at it. Nearing our stop
now, we're getting off at Bond Street,
we will never know

where you intend to take the heat
of all that passion, or what plans you have
in store for it, or indeed for whom
exactly it is being displayed

in this too-temporary moving room
where thrown together, interstellar,
bound by flesh and blood and bone-
bound, all of us are underground.

Orbit

Two blunt nothings
where nothing moves
are a surprise, alive
in the opacity of lake-
hill-mist-draped dawn.

I'm watching as a stare
spikes its orbit, a world
sized and measured
in the breath before
the hop-scotch skip.

The other hare just sits
and waits for what comes
next. Lost on soft feet, still
in the spin of my own life,
I head back to bed.

Notes

'The Blue Album', p.32

The songs alluded to in this sequence are:

1. An die Musik   (Schubert)
2. God Only Knows   (The Beach Boys)
3. Prime Time   (The Tubes)
4. O Mio Babbino Caro   (Puccini)
5. It's Too Late   (Carole King)
6. Blackbird   (The Beatles)
7. Angel from Montgomery   (John Prine)
8. You Keep Me Hangin' On   (The Supremes)
9. The Suburbs   (Arcade Fire)
10. One of These Things First   (Nick Drake)
11. Cornflake Girl   (Tori Amos)